D1060801

WE CELEBRATE CHRISTMAS IN WINTER

by Rebecca Felix

Cherry Lake Publishing • Ann Arbor, Michigan

Published in the United States of America
by Cherry Lake Publishing
Ann Arbor, Michigan
www.cherrylakepublishing.com

Consultant: Marla Conn, ReadAbility, Inc.
Editorial direction and book production: Red Line Editorial

Photo Credits: Shutterstock Images, cover, 1, 18; Narongrit Thongkam/Shutterstock Images, 4; iStockphoto/Thinkstock, 6; Sean Prior/Hemera/Thinkstock, 8; Kevin Smith/Design Pics/Corbis, 10; Stockbyte/Thinkstock, 12; Fuse/Thinkstock, 14; Randy Faris/Fuse/Thinkstock, 16; Jupiterimages/Thinkstock, 20

Library of Congress Cataloging-in-Publication Data
Felix, Rebecca, 1984-
We celebrate Christmas in winter / by Rebecca Felix.
pages cm. -- (Let's look at winter)
Includes index.
ISBN 978-1-63137-609-2 (hardcover) -- ISBN 978-1-63137-654-2 (pbk.) -- ISBN 978-1-63137-699-3 (pdf ebook) -- ISBN 978-1-63137-744-0 (hosted ebook)
1. Christmas--Juvenile literature. I. Title.

GT4985.5.F45 2014
394.2663--dc23

2014004490

Cherry Lake Publishing would like to acknowledge the work of The Partnership for 21st Century Skills. Please visit *www.p21.org* for more information.

Printed in the United States of America
Corporate Graphics Inc.
July 2014

TABLE OF CONTENTS

Merry
Christmas

Holiday

Christmas is a Christian holiday. It is in winter. It is on December 25.

What Do You See?

What treats do you see?

Treats and Trees

People get ready for weeks.
They bake treats.

What Do You See?

What is on the tree?

Families put up a **Christmas tree**. They **decorate** it.

Songs and Stories

People sing **carols**. They wear red or green.

People tell holiday stories.
Many are about Santa Claus.

Santa comes the night before Christmas. He travels the world. He brings gifts to children.

Give and Eat

Families and friends gather.
They **celebrate**. They give gifts.

What Do You See?

What foods do you see?

People eat a holiday meal.

Christmas is a time of joy. It is a time of giving.

Find Out More

BOOK

Prelutsky, Jack. *It's Christmas!* New York: HarperCollins, 2008.

WEB SITE

Christmas—Enchanted Learning

www.enchantedlearning.com/crafts/christmas/

Find crafts, quizzes, and printouts about Christmas.

Glossary

carols (KEHR-uhls) joyful songs sung during Christmas

celebrate (SEL-uh-brate) to enjoy an event or holiday with others

Christmas tree (KRIS-mus tree) an evergreen tree people put up in their homes at Christmas

decorate (DEK-uh-rate) adding color or objects to something

Home and School Connection

Use this list of words from the book to help your child become a better reader. Word games and writing activities can help beginning readers reinforce literacy skills.

bake
before
brings
carols
celebrate
children
Christian
Christmas
Christmas tree
comes
December
decorate
eat
families
foods
friends
gather
gifts
give
giving
green
holiday
joy
meal
night
people
put
ready
red
Santa Claus
sing
songs
stories
tell
time
travels
treats
wear
weeks
winter
world

What Do You See?

What Do You See? is a feature paired with select photos in this book. It encourages young readers to interact with visual images in order to build the ability to integrate content in various media formats.

You can help your child further evaluate photos in this book with additional activities. Look at the images in the book without the What Do You See? feature. Ask your child to describe one detail in each image, such as a food, activity, or setting.

Index

About the Author

Rebecca Felix is an editor and writer from Minnesota. She listens to carols for many weeks before Christmas. She puts up a Christmas tree and celebrates the holiday with her family.